Josiah Foster Flagg

Plastic filling and the basal principles

Josiah Foster Flagg

Plastic filling and the basal principles

ISBN/EAN: 9783337107932

Printed in Europe, USA, Canada, Australia, Japan

Cover: Foto ©Andreas Hilbeck / pixelio.de

More available books at **www.hansebooks.com**

PLASTIC FILLING

AND THE

BASAL PRINCIPLES OF THE "NEW DEPARTURE."

BY J. FOSTER FLAGG, D. D. S.,

FORMERLY PROFESSOR OF DENTAL PATHOLOGY AND THERAPEUTICS
IN PHILADELPHIA DENTAL COLLEGE.

PLASTIC FILLING, AND THE BASAL PRINCIPLES OF THE NEW DEPARTURE.

BY J. FOSTER FLAGG, D.D.S., OF PHILADELPHIA.

{ *New York Odontological Society.*
{ *Special Meeting, November 20th and 21st,* 1877.

The Society was called to order at 8 o'clock, P. M., November 20th, Dr. A. L. Northrop, President, in the chair. The essayist of the evening, Dr. J. Foster Flagg, of Philadelphia, spoke as follows:

MR. PRESIDENT, AND GENTLEMEN OF THE ODONTOLOGICAL SOCIETY OF NEW YORK: I wish to thank you from the very bottom of my heart for the invitation you have extended to me to speak to you this evening. I wish you to understand that I distinctly appreciate the honor which you have conferred upon me by giving me more than ten times the usual limit given to one who speaks before you. Furthermore, gentlemen, I know that you are well aware that I have much to present to you which is out of the ordinary course of communications to dental societies. But, gentlemen, you don't know half what a heretic I am! and as I think of the work before me I feel like a modern Daniel in a large-sized lion's den! I feel like an insignificant David before a full-sized Goliath; but as Daniel came out of the lion's den, and as Goliath went down before David, so I expect to get out unharmed, and so I expect Goliath to go down!

I have come here to-night to sling the first stone—not that I expect to hit him in the forehead—not that I by any means expect to *kill him* to-night, for he will die hard; but I do expect that strength will be given me to deal him a good, hard blow.

That which I bring you to-night is no growth of a day. It is no work of a year. I therefore recognize that what seems to me to sound as it ought to sound, will sound to you just as it ought not to sound. I shall present to you the time-honored and ordinarily "accepted creed" of dentistry, and I shall advocate before you the diametrically antagonistic "creed of the New Departure." Do you suppose it is a new thing for me to be antagonizing accepted dentistry? No, gentlemen, it is no new thing. For more than twenty years I have not known what it is to be upon the "right side."

Twenty years ago, my very good and highly esteemed friend, Prof. Robert Arthur, enunciated his belief in leaving decay in the cavities of teeth, and filling over it, for a wise and special purpose, as he thought, and it was stigmatized as nasty, dirty, slouchy work ; and our "great man," Prof. J. D. White, said that "when he could not spend time to properly clean out the cavities he would retire from practice." Here is a document written by my honored father's own hand, giving an account of the action of a college faculty on the question : "When the faculty of the old college met for the purpose of arranging the last 'Announcement' of that school, exception was taken by Prof. White to what he considered as 'false doctrine' on the part of Prof. Arthur in regard to two prominent features in our art, both of which may be considered of vital importance to our success as instructors, and to the successful practice of many of our graduates. The first of these was, that Prof. Arthur advocated the leaving of caries in the cavity of a tooth and plugging thereon ; and the second, deemed equally objectionable, that of using 'sponge gold' as a material for filling teeth, and as a substitute for gold foil. *Now, although every other member of the faculty fully coincided with Prof. White in his opposition to this practice of Prof. Arthur,*" etc., etc.

How many professors of to-day oppose the "leaving of decay and the plugging thereon" when the pulp would be exposed by its removal? How many? I ask ! *It is now the accepted practice ;* and yet, only twenty little years ago, it was so heretical and such "false doctrine," that the entire faculty "coincided with Prof. White ; " and Dr. Louis Jack and Dr. J. Foster Flagg were the only two men of the forty-five hundred dentists of the United States that immediately accepted Prof. Arthur's practice, and from that day to this have systematically left decay in every cavity where its removal would expose a living pulp. Thus you see it is no new thing for me to question the creed of the profession. I became used to it when I was young, and it has grown with my growth.

Years have rolled on, and, as you know, without much attendance on my part at dental meetings ; but do you suppose I have been doing nothing? Far from it. Day by day I have filled tooth after tooth, and have marked what I have done. Year by year I have tabulated results until they now amount to thousands upon thousands. Letters, by the score, have passed between Syracuse, St. Louis and Philadelphia. At length I wrote to my friends, Drs. Palmer and Chase, that I felt we were as ready now as ever we should be.

Gentlemen, we believe that we have for our "New Departure," grand, basal, foundation principles, which have so grown with us that they already seem as old and as solid as the hills. I don't come to say hard words to you ; I don't come to retort upon you for the language which some of you have used towards us. You who have said it know what you have said; but I come to ask, that *from this time on*, as we have spoken out our belief,—as we shall speak out our "creed,"—you will let us *believe* without saying *hard things of us.*

If you have any *good arguments* against our position, we are as anxious to hear them as you can possibly be to present them; but if you continue to say "plastering in amalgam," we could retort by saying, "punching and poking and pounding in gold," because we know that is the way it is done. But we also know that it cannot be *well* done in any other way; nor can plastic fillings be well put in without "plastering." It is the way to do it; and is not "plastering" quite as agreeable as "pounding?" We call your "punching and pounding" the *introducing* of the filling, and we wish you to call our "plastering" the *introducing* of our fillings.

More than twenty years ago, Prof. Elisha Townsend gave to his co-temporaries the assertion that he "saw daily the undeniable evidence of the fact that teeth could be saved with amalgam, which *he* could not save with gold." His memory is revered by us all. As a worker in gold he was unsurpassed. As a proof of his estimation of plastic filling, he gave to his profession "Townsend's Amalgam,"—that material with which we began our labors,—that material which had so much of good in it that we were more and more impelled, as the years passed by, to recognize its value.

I feel that I owe much to Prof. Townsend, for he made the way of experiment easy for me. Within a very short time after his death, nearly two hundred of his families became my patients. This not only placed me (then a beginner *in Philadelphia*) at once in full practice, but enabled me to cultivate a ground for plastic filling which had been well broken by one in whom they had unbounded confidence. Now, gentlemen, the statistics which I propose to offer to-night have been based upon this experience.

ARTICLE I. *Accepted Creed: Gold is the* BEST *thing to save teeth.*

ARTICLE I. *New Departure: In proportion as teeth need saving, gold is the* WORST *material to use.*

Gentlemen, I am, for the moment, literally but a mouth-piece. Dr. Chase has spoken to you. This article is his. He was the first who had the hardihood to say that "in proportion as teeth *need* saving, gold is the *worst* material to use." This he said, and Dr. S. B. Palmer and I fully endorse that which he has spoken.

Mark my words! This is a real *belief* which I am speaking to you. Men are coming to our belief every day—the thinking men, the observing men of dentistry. They write me that they introduce their beautiful jewels of gold with the view of their premature wreck staring them in the face! That with their very best, and long-continued effort, they are unable to save teeth as they would, *with gold*.

And is this nothing? Can a man continue to work, and put " piece after piece " in proper place when he feels that the work is killing the patient and himself too,—and that when a few short years shall have passed away, his work will be good for nothing?

This is what sapped me fifteen years ago. I had been filling teeth *then* for fifteen years. I can show you plenty of plugs of gold—not twenty or thirty — but hundreds, that I introduced more than twenty-five years since, and which are just as good to-day as on the day when they were done. But these were in strong teeth, in places easy and accessible, in teeth that might have gone but little had they been left unfilled; while of the others,—of the teeth that *needed* saving,—I can but tell you just what all have seen. One by one these teeth came back to me. Day by day I saw my best efforts going to destruction. I *heard* that my work must be defective ; but I *felt* that there *might be something lacking in the material.*

And then, there were the first of my statistics. It is more than twenty years since this work was begun. Twenty-two years ago I made five hundred fillings. Two hundred and fifty were of gold,— just as the cavities came in practice,—the next two hundred and fifty were filled with tin, gutta percha and amalgam,—the amalgam taking the brunt of the battle, and used in places that were too far gone for any other thing. I then waited for five years, watching the progress of events, and meanwhile returning to orthodox practice. At the end of this time I was not satisfied, and I waited another year. It was to be a *life-work* with me. I could not do it over again. Nor can I. I have done.

At the end of that time the "undeniable evidence" presented itself to my mind. I felt the truth of what Dr. Townsend had said, and came solidly to the belief that *I* could *save teeth* with amalgam which I *could not* save with *gold;* for, already in the soft teeth,—in the inaccessible places,—in the cavities under the gum and with frail walls,—the gold fillings were becoming defective ; while the plastic fillings, far, far better held their own.

To-day, gentlemen, the " efforts " in gold which formed that trial-band have almost passed away ; and still quite a number of the plastic fillings,—*some even of the most hopeless cases,*—are pointed to with pride, and satisfaction by their owners.

Seventeen years ago I began the systematic introduction of six per cent. of plastic fillings, choosing, of course, those places best adapted for them—that is, the *worst*. The next year I introduced twelve per cent. ; the next, eighteen per cent. ; and, year by year, results were such as warranted this progression. You can readily see where this ends. This is my seventeenth year, and I should have put in one hundred and two plastic fillings in every one hundred. I found myself not equal to the emergency!

I stand before you with a practice which I have been sixteen years in arranging. I have taken the refuse teeth from all directions; announcing, from year to year, to my patients, that I desired the teeth that were ordinarily extracted, and that I was fast abandoning artificial work, because I felt that I could do my patients better service by repairing wrecks and building crowns on roots. The result is, that I have many mouths in which the teeth have proven themselves wretched beyond wretchedness, yet these all are comfortable. I have teeth by the hundreds such as melt (for they *have* melted) from gold, like snow before the sun, at the hands of our very best operators.

For all this heap of seeming impossibility, I use nothing but plastic fillings. Once in a while I use *tin*, because I am engaged on a series of experiments to find the action of this metal on dentine. Our filling materials are, gutta percha, amalgam, and oxy-chloride of zinc (so-called). With these I do everything. All this in the mouths of the very best class of patients.

"*In proportion* as teeth *need* saving, gold is the *worst* material to use." This point alone takes in the whole of Palmer's electro-chemical theory of the action of filling materials: but I must tell you what the work of winnowing out the chaff, as far as we could do it, has eliminated.

The work has been done by Prof. Henry Morton, of Hoboken, and Prof. Snyder, of Philadelphia, scientists; Messrs. Eckfeldt and Du Bois, assayers of the Philadelphia Mint, metallurgists; and Drs. Palmer, Chase, and Flagg, dentists.

We have carefully, and, we believe, scientifically, investigated every line of experiment which has professed to *show* the *current* which, we believe, is eliminated by contact of metal with tooth-bone. This we have done with the best instruments and apparatus which our country can produce—and we find that such current *has never been shown*, much less measured. Even that curiously ingenious line of experimentation, upon this subject, which was presented at the "Centennial" meeting of the American Dental Association—and which gave to our profession that scale of relativity known as the "Harvard Tension Series," in which gutta percha was placed at "o" and gold at "200°," and which gave those who had faith in gold, such "a black eye" (as it was expressed) we pronounce utterly worthless and without any scientific basis. And yet,—I will read you Prof. Morton's opinion of that electro-chemical theory upon which we rest our belief as expressed in this Article I.; for, if gold *is* the worst material to use, there must be some scientific reason for it.

After speaking of the great difficulty of *current elimination*, Prof. Morton says,—" On the other hand, we have the best reason for assuming on analogy and authority that all chemical action invokes electric disturbance. Now acid fluids do act chemically on bone, and the presence of a good conductor, which is itself unattacked, in contact, must, on general electrical principles, assist the electro-chemical action. Supported by your facts of observation, and the reasonableness and consistency of the electric theory, you may well rest your case there. But it is, of course, very important not to give your opponents a chance to attack by resting, for a proof of your theory, on experiments which are themselves unsound and capable of confutation."

Now you see, gentlemen, that notwithstanding the fact that we are unable, as yet, to *demonstrate* the existence of the current, yet nevertheless, the "reasonableness" and "consistency" of our theory is such that we may say that gold, being a good conductor, and being itself unattacked, when placed in contact with tooth-bone, must on general principles cause excessive electro-chemical action, which action must eventuate in disintegration of tooth-tissue; and, therefore, gold is the *worst* material to use, when a tooth is of such structure and in such condition as that it needs something which will help to *preserve it*.

The stereotyped answer to this is couched in these few words,—" If gold is so put in as that no fluid can come between it and the tooth-bone, there will be no chemical action; because, where there is no fluid there cannot be any chemical action." Then, gentlemen, *why don't you put it in so?* If you cannot, then use something else, if for no other reason.

ARTICLE II. *Accepted Creed: Either "contour filling" or "separating teeth" is the best method to arrest decay.*

ARTICLE II. *New Departure: Neither "contouring filling" nor "separating teeth" has much to do with the arrest of decay.*

For years the discussion between contour and separation has gone on. With Arthur, Bonwill and Chupein, for the A, B, C, of the separationists, and Atkinson and Webb as representatives of the whole alphabetic list of contourists, (Atkinson even building Mansard roofs for the comfortable occupancy of the *tooth spirits*) and yet no definite decision has ever been reached. Now it seems to us that if either was, in truth, decidedly the right way, it would have been found out by this time.

In regard to this contest, *we* have been lookers-on, and our statistics do not yet show us which is best. Contour fillings fail, and fillings in separations fail; and when the contours fail, it is said, "It

ought to have been separated"; and when the fillings in the separa
tions fail, it is said, "The separation is not made rightly." Meanwhile, the teeth decay.

For me, in a strong, solid tooth, I would, for durability, just as
soon make a contour filling as I would a separation; but on general
principles, and for comfort, I prefer to give my patients the benefit of
what is called contour. My experience is that they are better than
the separations, certainly on the score of comfort, and probably on
the score of durability.

ARTICLE III.—*Accepted Creed. Failure in operations is mainly due to
defective manipulation.*

ARTICLE III.—*New Departure. Failure in operations is mainly due to
incompatibility of filling material with tooth bone.*

When I say to you that "failure in operations is mainly due to defective manipulation" does it not sound as though I was teaching
orthodox doctrine to young men?

We have striven to strengthen our efforts and to make them more
serviceable and acceptable to our patients by devising and using filling materials "compatible with tooth bone," but you are constantly
told that "*Excelsior*" is the word!

Did any of you ever hear that expression at a dental meeting?—
Did you ever hear any gentleman wind up a glowing peroration on
"fine work," "perfect manipulation," "conquering of all difficul-
ties," and "final glorious results" with "Excelsior! Gentlemen,
Excelsior is the word!"—Now what is this "Excelsior" business?—
It appears there was a young man climbing a mountain with a little
banner over his shoulder—He saw "nice, warm fires in happy homes"
and they made him "groan!" A worthy, reliable old gentleman
warned him against going further—but it was of no use, up he went!
A maiden requested him to "stop and rest his weary head upon her
breast;" and, do you believe it?—the fool wouldn't even stop for
that—and the end of it was that a dog found him dead in the snow!

Not any "Excelsior" for me!

But thus it is, all the elegant fillers, high style $75, $150, $500,
plug men tell you that failures are due to defective manipulation.
Now, gentlemen, if this is so, why don't you manipulate better? Simply because you cannot. And is it nothing against gold that men
cannot manipulate it? Is it nothing that this has been proven by an
experience of more than half a century? The record of to-day is not
better than the record of fifty years ago. You talk about the "finer
work," the "improvement in foil," the "improvement in instrumen-
tation," the "blessed rubber dam,"—but with all these adjuncts, while
you have put all these gifts to tests which have proven their greatest

capability, your results are, larger fillings, more difficult fillings, more tedious fillings, more painful fillings, more expensive fillings, less compensating fillings (both to yourselves and patients),—and *more decided failures.* I state this squarely. For every *one* of these large, difficult, tedious, painful and expensive fillings that have given a dozen years of service, I think you will acknowledge that I am within bounds when I say *a dozen* have proved failures.

My statistics show that the average of gold failures for the last year is greater than for any previous year. One hundred gold failures were classified upon my tables last year, for the whole twelve months; and this year, up to this month, I have already 86, making a total for 1877 of 103; many of them far worse failures. This is the truth. This shows what attempts are being made, and what failures are the results.

It was only on last Friday morning that I renewed (by guarding) a gold filling which had been introduced *less than three years* before, into a cavity upon the *mesial face of the right upper second bicuspid, with the first bicuspid out.* I want you to think of this, and note the exceeding difficulty (?) of the original operation. The patient, Mr. J. W., one of our largest car-wheel manufacturers, told me he paid $20 for the filling; and I showed him that I could pass a broad, thin instrument deep into the crevice between the filling and the tooth, at almost any point. I told him that *I could not say* of such beautiful work, what I believed the gentleman who did it, would say of it, viz. that it must have been *defective in manipulation;* but that I knew just how soft his teeth were (he had formerly been my patient,) and that I believed the failure was due to *incompatibility of gold with tooth bone.*

NOTE.—Since making the remarks and drawing the deductions (which are correctly published in the "Dental and Oral Science Magazine") in relation to this case, I have been informed by my patient that it was *not the $20 filling* which had failed, and that it had been introduced *three years and three months* instead of "*less than three years.*"

But while I eagerly embrace this opportunity to correct these errors, I would say that I could have cited plenty of cases which would have been *in principle* precisely as I represented this one, which was naturally first remembered in consequence of its recent reparation.

We believe that "failure in operations is mainly due to incompatibility of filling material with tooth bone." This again opens all the question upon which rests our vitality. When I tell you that *experimentally,* the contact of gold and bone, amalgam and bone, tin and bone, and gutta percha and bone, results, again and again, in greatest loss of substance in that bone which is in apposition with the *gold,*—I say, "he that hath eyes to see, let him see ; and he that hath ears to hear, let him hear." And when I see just the same thing occurring in the mouth, every day that I practice, and then read that "experiments out of the mouth must be taken for nothing !" I cannot but feel that such writers are "straining at gnats," while their patients are "swallowing camels."

ARTICLE IV.—*Accepted Creed: A tooth that is worth filling at all, is worth filling with gold.*

ARTICLE IV.—*New Departure : A tooth that can be so treated as to be satisfactorily filled with anything, is worth filling.*

The fourth article of the accepted creed and its twin brother " a tooth that can be filled at all, can be filled with gold," seem to me such perfect puerility that I have no patience with them. This latter enunciation is from our good friend Taft's last work on Dentistry,— "up to the present status of the profession," the preface says. The scathing criticism of this production in the "*Cosmos*" induced me to examine more closely than I might otherwise have done, this effort of Dr. Taft's. Among things like "vacuums" between pulp-caps and pulps, I found this statement, that "a tooth that is worth filling at all, is worth filling with gold." It is also enunciated that "a tooth that can be filled at all, can be filled with gold." So can a man walk from here to Broadway on his hands !—but it is not generally regarded as the best way to do it !

Neither is it the best thing always to fill any tooth that can be filled, with gold. It is not the best, the most acceptable, the most expeditious, or the most comfortable way to do. *It is not the most serviceable way to do.* I assert that experience proves this ; but beyond that, I most emphatically deny both assertions. I deny that "a tooth which cannot be serviceably filled with gold, is not worth filling." I deny that "any tooth which can be filled at all, can be filled with gold." No one, not even the most expert, can fill with gold every tooth that can be filled. How much less, then, can the average, respectable practitioners of dentistry do this thing? You may get gold into it, after a fashion, but you cannot fill it, according to your own ideal of what a filling should be.

On the other hand, with a plastic filling material it can be filled, and filled nicely, and so as to be comfortable and serviceable for many years. Experience has shown this. The profession, and the coming text-books, when they are truly "up to the status of the profession," will admit it. Therefore we say that " a tooth that can be so treated, as to be *satisfactorily* filled with *anything*, is worth filling."

ARTICLE V.—*Accepted Creed: Unskilled and unscrupulous dentists fill with tin covered with gold,* THEREBY *causing galvanic action, pulpitis, death of the pulp, abscess, and* LOSS OF THE TOOTH.

ARTICLE V.—*New Departure: Skillful and scrupulous dentists fill with tin covered with gold,* THEREBY *preventing decay and pulpitis and* THEREBY SAVING THE TOOTH.

"Unskilled" and "unscrupulous"—these are not nice words to use, and yet these are the words which, having been spoken and printed in relation to our practice, *compel* us to use the phrase "skillful and scrupulous"—and that is just what we mean—*if it is skillful,* to work out the *experimental* saving of teeth which in ordinary practice are lost—and, on the other hand, if it is not *scrupulous* to meet the indications more completely than had been done, and to *continue efforts in despite of the insinuations* that the *tin* was used because of its *cheapness !*—and the *gold as a means of hiding the deception !*—then I do not know what "scrupulous" means!

Experience had proven that tin would save teeth which gold did not. The accepted belief was, *and is,* that it did so because of its softness, and ease of manipulation,—(for which qualities, by the way, we have never heard it decried). *Our* belief now is, that it saves teeth because of its *low conductivity,* and because *it is itself attacked.* Experience had also proven that the tin wore out ; and so, the happy combination which would save the tooth and yet not wear out, having been devised, it was decried and defamed as *unskillful* and *unscrupulous.*

Fifteen years ago this was the accepted practice of my office. It is because of *this principle* that the operation of "guarding" with a crescentic guard of tin, amalgam, or gutta-percha at the "vulnerable spot" has retained failing gold plugs, by the hundred, for continued usefulness. I, myself, had, up to April, 1877, 1053 gold plugs, of my own, and many other operators', doing service *only* because they had been "guarded" in this way. Gold doing well because it was *taken care of* by *tin, gutta-percha,* or *amalgam !*—the *white* troops victorious, *because* the *colored* troops fought bravely !—a pretty picture.

ARTICLE VI. *Accepted Creed: A filling, to be good,* MUST NOT LEAK.

ARTICLE VI. *New Departure: A filling may be the* BEST *that is known for the tooth,* AND YET LEAK BADLY.

How do we maintain this point ? We hold that this is true because of the fact that gutta-percha makes a leaky filling. See this filling in this tube ; every care was taken that it should not leak. It was packed even better than it could have been in a tooth, and yet, as you see, it leaks badly. But you will say, that a glass tube is not analogous to a tooth. I am prepared for that. Here are small cups of ivory.

This material is almost identical with that of tooth bone These were filled, as you see, the one with red gutta-percha, and the other with Johnston's Premium Stopping ; and yet both leak.

Why do we maintain it ? We do so from the fact that *we wish to make it a basal principle, that mere leakage, itself, is not the thing* which makes a filling capable or incapable of *saving a tooth*. It depends upon what material leaks, and what it leaks in contact with. If a leak of vitiated saliva occurs between tooth bone and a material which is a *good conductor and is itself unattacked*, then that leaky filling is very bad. But if even vitiated saliva leaks between tooth bone and a material which is, practically, a non-conductor, and which has a surface that is *neither bright nor oxidizable*, then leakage is *proven* by *experience* to be *not* practically detrimental. This we hold to be the reason why gold fillings " eat themselves out " of soft teeth in from two to five years; and why gutta-percha remains untouched (except by attrition), and preserves such teeth for many, many years.

ARTICLE VII. *Accepted Creed : Gutta-percha*, PROPERLY USED, *is good enough for* TEMPORARY *fillings.*

ARTICLE VII. *New Departure : Gutta-percha*, PROPERLY USED, *is the* MOST PERMANENT *filling material we possess.*

When my friend, Dr. Hawes, was in my office for a part of two days, some months ago, I operated before him. Among other patients was a young lady from Orange, New Jersey. I showed him a line of several gutta-percha fillings, in front teeth, which had been introduced seven years before. I showed him a gutta-percha filling in the buccal face of a left lower molar, which he thought was " somewhat cupped," and would " hardly pass for a permanent filling." The patient informed him that it had been doing service for *twenty* or *twenty-one* years ! and I added, that if it lasted as much longer I should mark it down as permanent.

Twenty-six years ago, Dr. G., of Philadelphia, came to my father, desiring his services. My father introduced eleven gold fillings,— good, old-fashioned, solid, " straight from the shoulder " fillings. Beside these cavities there were four enormous places in the four *wisdom-teeth*, (poor teeth, according to "accepted" views), and these were filled, " experimentally ;" three with amalgam, and one (the buccal face of the right lower wisdom), with gutta-percha, with the idea that they might " last for a year or two." The last one of the eleven gold fillings was renewed a few months since, and the three amalgam fillings, *and the gutta-percha filling*, are still preserving their forlorn and worthless wisdom-teeth, as they have done, for *more than a quarter of a century !*

These are not isolated cases. They are, far more, *typical* cases. I have, in the mouths of my patients, hundreds upon hundreds of gutta-percha fillings, which have been doing service for from five to fifteen years, and bid fair to continue so doing for years to come.

Gentlemen, I feel, when I introduce a gutta-percha filling into a large cavity on the buccal, mesial, or distal face of a tooth,—close to the gum, with frail walls, and almost into the pulp, as though I had done something. I feel that I have (if it be possible) saved that tooth and pulp,—that I have placed there a material, which, even if it be gradually softened and worn out, will save the tooth until the last thin stratum, only, still remains. I feel that if it wears, an easy, inexpensive reparation can be effected, by the addition of a little more of the same material at any time. I feel that I have done my patient that real service which he or she had hoped to have bestowed.

This is why we say that "gutta-percha, properly used, is the most permanent filling material we possess."

ARTICLE VIII. *Accepted Creed: A* GOOD *gutta-percha filling,* IN ITS PROPER PLACE, *is better than a* POOR *gold one.*

ARTICLE VIII. *New Departure: A* POOR *gutta percha filling,* IN ITS PROPER PLACE, *is better than a* GOOD *gold one.*

This seems almost like a joke!—but we have introduced this as an "emphatic," and we mean just what we say.

Some time ago, a few of our Philadelphia gentlemen saw themselves on paper as saying almost too much in favor of gutta-percha ; so they corrected it by publishing that they did not mean to say that gutta-percha was as good as gold ; what they meant was, " that a real good gutta-percha filling, *in its proper place,* was better than a poor gold one." Meanwhile, cases such as this were coming to our notice. Mr J. G. W. had a gold filling introduced upon the mesial face of the left upper lateral, by one of our best operators. In about two years the filling failed. It was renewed, and in less than two years this second filling failed. We think we have a right to infer that both these fillings were good ones. Upon the occasion of a third visit, a gutta-percha filling was hastily introduced, to serve merely, *as was stated,* a temporary purpose. While yet the filling was in place, the gentleman's partner (a patient of mine) induced him to call upon me. I was told the story. I examined the gutta-percha filling. It bore evidence of its hasty insertion, having overhanging edges. These I trimmed with a warm instrument, and asked him to give me the first proof of his confidence in his partner's recommendation and my judgment by allowing the gutta-percha filling to remain, as it was a *proper place* for it. Already that filling has lasted longer than either of the gold ones, and, from appearances, it will last far longer than both the gold ones together.

This is also not an isolated case, and it is from such instances as these that we deduce " that a *poor* gutta-percha filling, *in its proper place*, is *better* than a *good* gold one !"

ARTICLE IX. *Accepted Creed:* **Amalgam,** PER SE, *is a* POOR *filling material.*

ARTICLE IX. *New Departure: Amalgam,* PER SE, *is an* EXCELLENT *filling material.*

I do not mean to say that all you gentlemen think or say that amalgam is a poor filling material. But I do mean that this is the teaching of the most recent and accepted text-books and authorities. Read Taft, pages 93, 94 and 95, and you will see the "creed" of "Ann Arbor" and "Ohio."

I am truly thankful, for the sake of conservative dentistry that such teachings are hemmed in on the West by St. Louis! and on the East by Syracuse and Philadelphia !—and for the whole matter of the three pages devoted to the discussion of amalgam, I assure you, gentlemen, it is entirely NOT so !—Not but that the author believes what he has written, not but that he conscientiously believes every word of it. But from the washing of the mass in "*boiling water*" who ever heard of such a thing? much more, who ever saw it done? to the final statement that " the cohesive property of gold renders this metal equal in adaptability to amalgam " (!) it is *practically* all NOT so. Read it, gentlemen, read it, and don't believe it !—"Amalgam, *per se*, is an *excellent* filling material."

Nevertheless, I do not wish you to think for a moment, that we regard amalgam as the ULTIMA THULE. *By no means. While we recognize its great excellence, we also recognize its great deficiencies.*

The relative durability of the three materials,—gutta percha, amalgam, and gold,—is a question which I have been engaged upon for more than fifteen years; during which period I have endeavored to tabulate this matter by following the career of over *twenty thousand* fillings. Of course, I recognize the impossibility of *doing* this *with scientific* accuracy. I admit that my result is merely a guess; but, gentlemen, I regard it as a *very close guess*, that as the result of *average dentistry*, gold fails in fifteen years in seventy-one per cent. of its cases, and amalgam in fifty-four per cent. of its cases. Understand me, this is *average* dentistry. It is not *poor* dentistry, for the gold efforts of such, you know, would not nearly reach such a standard. Neither is it truly "first-class" dentistry. If it were, I should be ashamed of first-class dentistry. But it is very close to what our Profession, as a Profession, is doing for those of humanity at large who come to us for services.

Now when you reflect that all the good places, all the easy places, all the accessible places, as a rule (admitting all exceptions) are filled with gold; and that all the bad places, all the hard places, all the "forlornities," as a rule (admitting the exceptions) are filled with amalgam,—*we* think that it does not tell so badly for amalgam, while we say for the gold, that it is a pity that it is so incompatible with tooth-bone.

For gutta-percha, with two thousand fillings of an average duration of eight years, (these were in carefully selected places, but all in *soft* teeth) the failure is but eight per cent. One hundred and sixty failures in soft teeth, in two thousand cases, in eight years. These failures were mostly from disintegration of the gutta-percha. The action of the fluids of some mouths causes this material to soften, puff up, and disintegrate. In such mouths gold is almost worthless for the average practitioner, except upon the articulating faces of the teeth; and, in these mouths, tin and amalgam have proved themselves our most reliable filling materials.

But you will say that gutta-percha fillings do not ordinarily last that way. That is because they are put in definitely, only as temporary work, being removed in a short time to be replaced with work which is *called* permanent. The gutta-percha is almost always found (no matter how long it has been allowed to remain), *preserving the tooth* perfectly; and is frequently complimented by the operator for having done so, even while he is introducing his permanent filling,—which, in truth, has often to be renewed sooner than would have been the case had he allowed his temporary filling to have remained.

Again, your instructions as to working gutta-percha, from the directions to "heat it on a porcelain or metal slab over a spirit-lamp," (there is no surer method of ruining the material from over-heating) to the "holding of an instrument on the filling, and pressing it till it is cool"; these instructions, I think, amount to nothing. Take a cavity on a lower second molar, first molar and wisdom tooth in place. The cavity shall begin on the mesial face, and deeply circumscribe the tooth, close to and partially under the gum, until it has passed along the buccal and distal faces and impinged a little on the lingual face. There is a place to fill! You all have seen such places, and they are excellent to fill with gutta percha.

I have often listened to good friend Atkinson, as, with streams of intelligence scintillating from his flashing eyes, and his whole countenance beaming with enthusiasm, he would expatiate on the wonderful workings of the mallet in the "hands of intelligence." But I tell you, gentlemen, it would take no less than *four instruments* in the hands of *four intelligences* to press in such a plug *till it got cold!*

ARTICLE X. *Accepted Creed: The use of "plastic" filling materials tends to lower the standard of Dentistry, thereby diminishing its sphere of usefulness.*

ARTICLE X. *New Departure: The use of "plastic" filling materials tends to lower that Dentistry which has for its standard of excellence "ability to make gold fillings," but very much extends the sphere of usefulness of that Dentistry which has for its standard of excellence "*ABILITY TO SAVE TEETH.*"*

This is where we rest our case. It is for the *salvation of teeth* that I have come to speak to you to-night. I have spoken only with that end in view. I don't wish to speak of good, strong teeth. I don't wish, *at this time*, to tell you of my practice of to-day,—what I am experimenting on,—what I am tabulating. I have come only to tell you what I *have done*, and what conclusions I have arrived at, as the result of experience and long years of practice.

But I do not wish to say anything to you of the teeth which you are in the habit of filling successfully, and, as we express it, satisfactorily, with gold ; teeth of dense structure, whose cavities have walls so strong that you can impact a filling which lasts a lifetime. But I do ask that you will gradually discontinue this packing of gold into teeth that are so poor, so frail, so unsubstantial that it is, to say the least, doubtful whether the result will be creditable to your profession, or satisfactory to your patients.

Commence, if you will, with those poorer and more miserable teeth which you would condemn to the forceps, and fill them with plastic fillings. I desire that you shall *do it well*—just as your trained hands can do it *after you have learned*. Take this just as I mean it, gentlemen, for, is it not "reasonable" and "consistent" that if you had filled largely with plastic materials and but little with gold, you would not fill to the best advantage with gold; *therefore*, as you have filled largely with gold, and but little, comparatively, with plastic materials you will not, at first, fill to the best advantage with plastics. But you will soon be agreeably impressed with your results in the new direction. You will soon find that much which has been told you by tradition and text books has no reality in it. It is true that our results are produced more easily, comfortably and economically to the patients, but they will not complain of that. It is also true that our results are produced with greater ease to the operator ; and, for this reason, it is argued by our opponents that we do it from "laziness."

But I tell you, that it is not from laziness. It is from a desire to lay aside the forceps. It is from a desire that our patients shall eat upon teeth, the roots of which, at least, are in their jaws. It is from a desire that they shall be exempt from the infliction of artificial work. It is from a desire to extend the blessings which the hand of our profession holds to bestow. It is that we may be sought, rather than avoided, that we may be extolled rather than decried, that we may be esteemed rather than censured, that rather than be feared, we may be loved and *respected*. It is for this that I have worked ; and blessed be God ! that He has so sustained and directed me that I have, every day, fresh cause to believe that I have gained the love of my patients. and the respect of my professional brethren !

And now, I find on the programme "Incidents of Practice." I supposed it meant "incidents of *my* practice," and so I have come prepared with a few to offer you !

Since twelve years ago (July 1865) I have been keeping the money record of five sets of teeth,—among the softest and frailest of those under my charge. These were poor enough ; decayed through and through, so that you could *string* five or six in a row ; broken off, decayed down to and under the gum. From 1865 to 1877 (twelve years) these teeth have been kept, comfortably, in order. Not *one* tooth has been lost from the five mouths, during all this time. That alone, is something ; but in adding up the aggregate of all their bills, and dividing the total by five, it shows that those mouths have been kept in order for less than $15 each per year ($14.80). This brings dentistry within the reach of many who have heretofore been deprived of its benefits. It brings it where it belongs, to be a blessing to the millions ; and this is why we say that our "practice" very much extends the sphere of usefulness of that dentistry which has for its standard of excellence "ability to save teeth."

Prof. J. G. Richardson had in 1869 a right upper lateral, right upper central, and left upper central decayed and needing saving. The lateral and left central were filled with gold ; but the right central, being much worse than either of the others, my advice was asked in regard to it before it was filled. I said that it would be best to fill it with gutta-percha. "What ! a front tooth ?" was the reply. "Why, yes ! why not ?" said I ; "a man wants to save his front tooth just as much as he would a back one !" So it was filled with gutta-percha. In a few months from that time the lateral ached so badly during an entire night, that, in the morning (I think it was on Sunday—I was not in the city), he called upon a dentist and insisted that it should be extracted. In the course of time an ominous shadow passed over the left central, which told that its pulp had quietly died a natural death. It was entered, the pulp removed, and it is now doing good service as a pulpless tooth. But the *worst of the three*, the one that in 1869 most *needed* saving, *has been saved*, and is, to-day, a living, healthy, brilliant tooth. I saw it but a few days since. The filling is a little worn. I have an appointment with him, to add a little gutta percha to it, on my return; when, with fifteen minutes' work, I shall start it off for another eight or ten years' journey.

Mrs. McG., left upper lateral: In this tooth two gold fillings, one $5, the other $6, lasted fifteen years. By the failure of both the tooth had become pretty badly decayed. *Twelve* years ago a gutta-percha filling was introduced for $4. With two trifling repairs—so trifling as to cost nothing,—that filling has preserved the tooth perfectly.

Mrs. B., eleven years ago, had a range of gutta-percha fillings introduced by a gentleman in Germantown. Her teeth were very frail. The fillings cost $25. In about two years, while visiting one of our Philadelphia gentlemen, she mentioned that it was about two years since she had had any work done. She requested an examination, and was told, *very emphatically*, that there was some great mistake, that there was nothing but *temporary work* in her mouth, and that *she* ought not to have any other than the *very best*, which was *gold work*. Rather shocked at what she heard, she immediately made appointments, and had over $150 worth of gold fillings introduced.

All the gutta-percha fillings were removed and replaced with gold, *except one poor molar;* which was stated to be "worth nothing except gutta-percha." In about two years from that time she visited my office at the recommendation of a friend, when I found every gold filling in such condition that my friend, Dr. Dixon, would have thought proper to have them removed. I said to her that the mistake had been made of filling her teeth with *gold*, when they ought to have been filled with *gutta-percha;* and, showing her the *poor molar*, said, "Do you see, this poorest of all the teeth has been filled with gutta-percha, and it is the only one that is not very defective."

Her eyes filled with tears as she told me the story of her four years' experience; and, as she finished, she asked what she should do. I suggested that she should call on and show the gentleman who did the gold work the result of his labors. This proposition being declined with a show of considerable spirit, I then suggested that she should let the first gentleman replace the defective fillings with gutta-percha, as he had had the good judgment to do it in the first place. She said that he was in Florida, and would not be back until some months later, and then asked if I would fill them with gutta-percha. I did so; and some three years after (she had gone to the far West), I heard that all was comfortable and doing well.

Just $200 for $25 worth of work!—as one practical experience of gold fillings in soft teeth!

Dr. S. has three daughters. The eldest had centrals and laterals filled with gold at nine years of age. These fillings failed and were renewed when she was eleven. Again they failed, and at **thirteen** and fourteen years of age they were severally renewed. Under these fillings the pulps died, and the teeth came to me for treatment. She has four discolored, pulpless teeth.

The teeth (centrals and laterals) of the second daughter were filled when she was nine with malleted fillings. At eleven they failed, when hand pressure fillings were introduced. These failed when she was between thirteen and fourteen, and gutta-percha fillings were then introduced. At sixteen these are good, and all the pulps are vital.

The centrals and laterals of the third daughter were filled with gutta-percha when she was nine. She is now twelve, and all the fillings are just as they were when introduced.

These are typical cases of my gutta-percha results. Now for amalgam.

Mr. D., the great umbrella manufacturer of our city, came to me in 1859 with a left upper molar. It had been pronounced unworthy of salvation, and he desired ether as an anæsthetic. I suggested that it would be a very great loss to him, and proposed treating it and building on an amalgam crown. This was done, and to-day he calls it his "veteran;" and it has enlisted many a new recruit into my army of teeth "not worth saving!"

Mr. C. W. came to me in 1857, with no teeth to spare. He was in young middle life (twenty-seven or eight), and had already lost many teeth. The tooth he came to have extracted was filled then with amalgam. He broke the crown off a *few weeks since*. I show it to you here. The roots have a full amalgam crown built on them now, of "Eckfeldt & Du Bois' Standard Alloy."

Since 1857 I have a list of a few over 500 patients who have come to me having lost already what teeth they could comfortably spare; and from all these mouths, since that time, *not one tooth has been extracted*. Can any of you do any better than that with your $40 gold fillings?

Now I have here three teeth which I have brought you on the *discoloration* question. I would have brought more, but *unfortunately* the patients are eating on them! This one was in service 15 years; this one for 17 years; and this one for 22 years. Do you see that these teeth are *not one particle discolored?* These fillings are made of Townsend's Amalgam, which contains only tin and silver. When such fillings leak sufficiently, the tooth becomes discolored,—just as teeth become discolored when gold fillings leak; but so long as they are tight, and in teeth of average quality as to structure, then discoloration is the *rare exception*, rather than the rule. I tell you, let an *average* operator introduce into one hundred *average* teeth, fifty fillings of gold and fifty fillings of amalgam, and in ten years there will not only be more of the amalgam fillings doing good service, but among the fillings that are left, there will be found more discoloration around the gold fillings than are around those of amalgam. This is a startling statement, at least to some of you; but I assure you that I do not make it loosely, but as the result of long and careful watching,— as the result of many years of patient observation. Try it, those of you who doubt, and see for yourselves. For me, I am far beyond *trying* this now. I practice solidly upon this belief every day.

Again, your ideas of amalgam are based almost exclusively upon its workings in the enormous cavities of almost completely abandoned teeth. You select teeth that, you say, are " worthy of nothing else." Now is this fair ? For if amalgam will save such teeth *even doubtfully well and exceptionally*, is it not worthy a trial in some of the *moderately sized* cavities of teeth of *somewhat better structure*, where, even yet, gold *occasionally* fails ?

It was said on one occasion, by my very good friend Dr. Bogue, that he " viewed with admiration the pin-head cavities in centrals filled with amalgam by Dr. Clowes." Now I have viewed, I think, a great deal more frequently, with *not* so much admiration, the *enormous* cavities in centrals which *had become so* (I say this advisedly) as the result of two or three consecutive gold fillings in each. For me, I would rather have one of Dr. Clowes' "pin-head " amalgam fillings in one of my centrals, than to have one of those evidences of "first-class ability " such as carried death to the pulps of both centrals and laterals of the young lady whose case I have related to you this evening.

Nor, gentlemen, is this any unusual story of "accepted " dentistry. Front teeth, *par excellence*, are filled and refilled with gold, as the *best* that can be done, until pulp after pulp dies, tooth after tooth becomes discolored and crumbles away, root after root is extracted, and plate after plate is inserted. This is *stereotyped practice*, and I defy contradiction of the statement.

I think that a liberal allowance of gutta-percha and amalgam fillings in these very teeth, while yet the cavities are *only pin-head cavities*, would be *a step in advance of this!*

This is *still* talk—*it makes quiet*—but it is what I have come tonight to say.

Now, gentlemen, I want to tell you one thing more which has grown out of our Plastic Fillings,—that we have not come before you prepared for only a small struggle. We are prepared for the fight. We feel that we have plenty of shot in the locker. We have opened our batteries against the accepted dentistry of the day. We are an aggressive party, and we purpose *insisting* that our " Basal Principles " shall be thoroughly discussed. We purpose making it *respectable* that teeth shall be filled with materials that experience has shown to be able to save them; and we purpose making it *not respectable* to fill teeth with materials that experience proves daily to be "unequal to the emergency."

Gentlemen, I have brought up thirteen hundred patients from childhood; and from the whole thirteen hundred mouths but *five* permanent teeth have been extracted, and these five teeth I have as the trophies of my success: not to show that my "scalps" are many, but to glory that they are so few. I do not say this to you boastfully. I could not do that, for my heart is too full of earnest, deep-seated thankfulness that it has been given to me to go in that path which has led to so much comfort for so many of my fellow-creatures. But I must plead guilty to a feeling of the intensest satisfaction as I think of the fact that every one of *mine* eat upon full, unbroken arches, above and below!

Gentlemen, make a beginning with the teeth you would extract, and treat them. Make *that* dentistry. Fill them with plastic fillings; and if, in twenty years, your experience shall have been that which mine has been, you will thank that great and excellent dentist, Elisha Townsend, as I thank him, for having had the hardihood to break the trammels of tradition and authority in declaring that "teeth could be saved with amalgam which *he* could not save with gold."

And now, as in conclusion I again thank you for having listened to my long effort, how vividly comes to my mind the parable of the sower and the seed—I feel that I have been sowing the seed to-night —some has fallen by the wayside and the birds have already picked it up—some has fallen upon stony ground and will spring up quickly, but having little earth it will soon wither away—some will fall among tares, and the tares will grow up and choke it—but I have faith to believe that yet some has fallen upon good ground, and that *in due time*, this will bring forth fruit, some thirty, some sixty-fold, and some an hundred.

"IN ABSENTIA,"

BY

J. FOSTER FLAGG, D. D. S.,

PHILADELPHIA, PA.

The New York Odontological Society held its regular meeting on Tuesday evening, April 10th, 1888, in the parlors of the New York Academy of Medicine, No. 12 West Thirty-first street.

The President, Dr. J. Morgan Howe, in the chair.

The President. We will now pass to the consideration of the subject of the evening :—

"METALS AND OTHER MATERIALS FOR FILLING TEETH."

This is intended to include a discussion of the subjects of gutta-percha and amalgam, and especially the papers of Drs. Flagg and Bonwill, which there was not time to discuss at their reading. As Dr. Flagg's paper was the more recent and is fresher in our minds, we will consider that and the subject of gutta-percha first. I will ask Dr. Payne to favor us with what he has to say on the subject of gutta-percha.

Dr. E. T. Payne. The address delivered at our last meeting by Prof. Flagg would have been more profitable, it appears to me, if his remarks had been formulated for a paper which could have been read in forty minutes or one hour. Members could then have asked questions and brought out points which would have been instructive, and, I am inclined to think, more profitable than the protracted talk.

After eliminating the cavities where the speaker said gutta-percha was not indicated as a desirable filling for permanency, there can be no controversy as to its being the most permanent and useful filling for the class of cavities selected for its use. It confirms the judgment of men of experience—nothing more. Prof. Flagg distinctly said he did not want the material looked upon as a crutch to help us over difficult places, and spoke disparagingly of Dr. Atkinson, who had recommended it in that relation. His teaching in respect to this point will not be accepted by those practitioners who have kept sensitive, low-toned teeth quiet and comfortable with gutta-percha until something more permanent could be used. If young men do accept such teaching they will deny themselves a great help to usefulness.

I heartily indorse all that was said about using steam heat in preparing the filling for the cavity, and the heating of instruments also. Too much care cannot be taken in this matter. Heating any gutta-percha stopping over the flame of a lamp is bad practice, and generally results in more or less injury to the filling. Dr. Hill once told me he was convinced comparatively few dentists used gutta-percha in such a way as to obtain the best result. My experience induces me to indorse what he said so many years ago.

Regarding the longevity of gutta-percha fillings, I want to say that undoubtedly it is true that in a few instances fillings made of gutta-percha remained in teeth twenty years or more. Prof. Flagg left it a fair inference that the same result would obtain now if the case was favorable and a good quality of gutta-percha was properly used. The inference is *misleading* and *untrue*.

In a paper on gutta-percha read before this society four years ago, I stated that the gum obtained by cutting the tree and scraping the inside of the bark was much superior to any obtained by tapping. It is to that superior quality of gum—which Dr. Hill used the first years of his experience—that the results so much talked about are due. The specimens displayed by the speaker, both the crude and that which was prepared for the teeth, are the product of tapping. Fillings made in the best manner with such material will not last longer than from two to eight years. Very few, indeed, will last more than four. Let us not deceive ourselves. It cannot be depended upon as formerly. The reason is the inferiority of the base. A fountain does not rise above its source.

I object to the speaker's position in claiming so much for the material. It is very useful, and the cause is weakened by claiming too much. Young practitioners should be taught these facts instead of accepting the fair inference from Professor Flagg's remarks that if his steam-made stopping is used all will go well for from five to thirty years. His statement that red gutta-percha shrinks more than any other may be proved by test-tubes, but my experience proves that it will last longer than the average stopping. One reason is it has less foreign substance incorporated into it. Pure gum would outlast any other, and if it could be used to advantage, it would be almost perfect as to its lasting qualities. Its color, however, is objectionable.

I repeat what I said in my paper four years ago, that, just in proportion as the particles are separated by a foreign substance, just in that proportion is the substance weakened both in strength and in ability to resist the fluids of the mouth

We were told by Prof. Flagg that it is our duty to test the material before using it, as one can do so in a few minutes in his office. A little farther on we are told that so difficult is an analysis of the material that it is not known positively what substance Hill incorporated with his base. His statement that Hill's formula is unknown, because he did not happen to know it, is suggestive and amusing, to say the least. There was no intimation that gutta-percha stopping was not in every way as good now as it was twenty-five or thirty years ago when Hill and Bevans were using the gum before referred to. He knew, of course, that the best stopping in the market to-day is very much inferior to the article which gave the filling material its deservedly high reputation From such a source of learning and respectability we had a right to look for the whole picture. His assertion, for instance, that a good stopping cannot be made without steam heat, porcelain slabs, etc., is a dogmatic assumption which he refutes when he further says Hill's stopping lasted thirty years, etc. Hill never used steam heat.

From my experience with the preparation of the material I am confident steam heat is better than dry heat and kneading-sticks. But to say that good results cannot be obtained in the old way is not true. I experimented all one winter to make an improvement in the texture of the manufactured material, as there was such an evident falling off in quality, and I found the whole trouble was with the base. Until the material can be obtained as it used to be, by cutting the tree, I propose to use the filling for what it is worth, as I find it, not expecting too much from it, or what was once realized.

The President. The next contribution to the subject of the evening will be a paper by Dr. Bogue, which he will kindly read now.

Dr. E. A. Bogue then read the following paper, entitled :—

"FILLING MATERIALS AND METHODS,"

in which, after referring to materials and methods, he continued as follows :—

"I think we all owe our thanks to Dr. Flagg for his late discourse on gutta-percha, and especially for the clear way in which he has defined the class of cases where its use as a filling for decayed teeth is indicated. His enthusiasm leads him to say some things, however, that ought to be challenged. If he is right, it can be proven; if wrong, it is the function of this society to point it out.

"As one person, I regret that Dr. Flagg felt it necessary to excuse himself for the exclusive use of plastics, or that he cited the fact of his presence before this society as an 'evidence that he had maintained his respectability.' He ought not to need any such evidence. It has been the maxim of this society to 'prove all things, and hold fast that which is good.' So all men having ideas to present have been welcomed.

"It has been Dr. Flagg's effort for more than twenty years, of my personal knowledge, to save teeth that many other practitioners would extract. The good that he has accomplished commands sincere respect; but I cannot say as much for some of his statements and some of his methods. I regret to hear such words as these: 'I want to induce you to try these things, for certainly you must understand that you know little or nothing about plastic fillings. You may have been told that my practice is among the rag-tag and bob-tail from the gutters of Philadelphia, but you know very well that my patients are among the very best, the most intelligent, and the most wealthy of the people of that city, and are typical individuals of their class ; and yet they are perfectly satisfied with the work I do for them.'

"Comforting the declining years of aged people, even if they are millionaires or members of the best society, by preserving their natural teeth, using the gentlest possible means, whether those means be gutta-percha or amalgam, is praiseworthy. But can we denominate as praiseworthy and strictly scientific a sentence like this: 'If *I* do not know when it is best to extract a tooth, I do not know which of you does.' Or a question so misleading as this: 'If you place your gutta-percha, properly prepared, where little or no wear can come upon it, in such wise that you know just as well as you know anything that a zinc-phosphate filling would not have lasted two little years, a gold filling would not have lasted five years, an amalgam filling would not have lasted more than ten years, and your gutta-percha filling lasted fifteen years,—then I ask of you if gutta-percha properly used is not the most permanent filling material we possess?' Dr. Flagg leads up to an answer which he seems to desire, but it should be recognized that his premises are not generally to be admitted without question, hence his inferences are often fallacious. Very few men, except Dr. Flagg, have seen many gutta-percha fillings fifteen years old, and Dr. Flagg himself is greatly elated by coming across such fillings. In such cases, undoubtedly it was the best material.

"But when Dr. Flagg's next sentence asserts interrogatively that gutta-percha, properly used, is the most permanent filling we possess, I think his enthusiasm would make his hearers infer more than he actually means; particularly when he continues by saying, 'I want to leave with you to-night the impression that you can work gutta-percha precisely the same as you work cohesive gold.' Yet farther on he admits the value of copper amalgam in desperate cases. Dr. Flagg counsels us to 'have our gutta-percha tested, so that we know exactly what it is composed of and the proportions of it," and he says "any man can test it in ten minutes in his office.' Three minutes later Dr. Flagg says: 'We have known positively for half a century that Hill's gutta-percha stopping was not made of quicklime and silex, but do not know what it was made of. So difficult is its analysis that we have not been able to say positively what Dr. Hill made his stopping of.' A little later in his address Dr. F. says: 'The only way for you to use gutta-percha successfully is to test the various materials before putting them into the mouth. It is the work of a life-time.'

"'Ten minutes' have lengthened into 'half a century,' and half a century into a life-time very quickly—but, as Dr. Flagg says he tells 'the truth, the whole truth, and nothing but the truth,' we must seek to reconcile these conflicting statements as best we may.

"Dr. Flagg says next: 'I do not want *my* material to be looked upon as a crutch.' He will, it is hoped, pardon the suggestion that this society was not aware that gutta-percha was a proprietary article, and it must regard all subjects brought before it as absolutely free for discussion. Dr. Payne asked how Dr. Flagg accounted for the protection of the tooth against decay when the shrinkage of a gutta-percha filling necessarily admits more or less moisture to the cavity, when disintegration of tooth would ensue if a gold filling leaked? (Please notice Dr. Payne's admission of the correctness of the general belief that a leaky gold filling will allow disintegration of tooth-substance around it.) Dr. Flagg replied that the gutta-percha was a non-conductor of galvanic or electric currents, and that, *therefore*, no chemical action takes place between the gutta-percha and the tooth-bone. He says the only action that can take place is the leakage of moisture.

"Dr. Flagg, speaking of amalgams, says that 'amalgam permits moisture to do good.' He claims to recognize that fact, and, therefore, says that 'amalgams that do not shrink are not as good tooth-savers as amalgams which shrink.' He has much to say about tooth-savers, meaning fillings. His practice necessarily leads to inaccuracies both in excavation and in adaptation of filling materials. He has invited the worst class of cases and the worst class of teeth. As it would be a physical impossibility to use gold in most of those cases, Dr. Flagg has elected to use plastics in all of them. The results obtained are the sum of his experience. This experience, though strictly empirical, is most valuable, but it does not justify any one in dogmatic assertions that he cannot prove. All this galvano-electric current assertion comes under that head.

"If Dr. Flagg could be induced to answer concisely, according to his knowledge, he would agree that the causes of decay in teeth, leaving out of view heredity, which would have to do with form and position, may be summed up in very few words, viz.: that which causes solution. Now, solution of the enamel never takes place at any point where it is exposed to friction, but only in such spots or crevices as favor the retention of foreign substances which, under the combined influences of heat, moisture and atmospheric contact, speedily produce disintegrating acids in a nascent condition. The experienced dentist knows full well where to look for dental decay. The smaller the crevice the longer it takes for the enamel to break down, but Dr. McQuillen showed many years ago how, between two plates of sound enamel, the substances that produce decay may reach the dentine, and so largely disintegrate it as to cause almost total destruction of the crown before the patient is conscious of disease. How, then, can we be told that leakage is a benefit? How can those amalgams that contract be vaunted as the best? How can gutta-percha be regarded as anything else than a valuable adjunct to our various filling materials?

"We must necessarily challenge the statement that 'amalgams that do not shrink are not as good tooth-savers as amalgams whichs hrink,' for both palladium and copper are recognized as being the best preventives of decay among all the amalgams, yet these two do not shrink. Dr. Flagg himself counsels copper amalgam in desperate cases.

"Dr. Flagg goes on to say: 'In five minutes you can tell whether an amalgam will shrink or not.' This is absolutely incorrect in regard to any strange or new amalgam. I have tested several amalgams that have continued to change their form for several days, sometimes shrinking, sometimes expanding.

"I think Dr. Flagg scarcely meant that he could ascertain in thirty minutes the composition of a new amalgam; still less its quantitative composition. Yet one might infer that from his saying that he could ascertain its composition in thirty minutes.

"In advocating gutta-percha for front teeth, Dr. Flagg failed to state that this material often becomes so dark on the surface as to be more unsightly than many amalgams, and always changes color, becoming fluffy or soiled.

"Having thus called attention to a few of the inconsistencies and errors in Dr. Flagg's address, I beg to call attention to another portion of that same address which contains the most precise, accurate and concise description of where and when to use gutta-percha that I have ever heard: 'Gutta-percha is not presented as a material suitable for all sorts of cavities, but only those having circumscribed walls—comparatively round, shot-hole cavities in the buccal, distal and mesial surfaces of teeth, not on the articulating surfaces; where the cavity is small on the outside and large on the inside, and where the tooth is soft, of frail structure and highly organic; such cavities as would be prepared for gold filling by cutting away all the surrounding enamel walls until you get to strong walls—in filling such cavities with gutta-percha you conserve the enamel structure all that you possibly can.' If you add frail and loose teeth and badly leaning ones to this category, it epitomizes the best features of the paper."

   *   •   *   •   *

Dr. Perry. One good result of Dr. Flagg's lecture is the most

excellent paper that we have just listened to from Dr. Bogue. I am in accord with almost every sentiment that he has uttered on that subject.

REPLY.

"IN ABSENTIA."

BY J. FOSTER FLAGG D. D. S., PHILADELPHIA, PA.

Honors conferred in this fashion are sometimes creditable and sometimes discreditable alike to donors and recipients. If creditable, then all is well, but if discreditable, either to donors or recipients, then all is not well.

At the meeting of the New York Odontological Society, held February 14th, 1888, I had the pleasure of speaking in behalf of gutta-percha stopping, and, after two months had passed, at a meeting of the same Society, held April 10th, 1888, reported in July *Cosmos*, p. 475, Drs. E. T. Payne, and E. A. Bogue gave utterance to comments upon my effort which are so discreditable to themselves, and which, if true, would be so discreditable to me that I deem it my duty to reply at once.

First, for Dr. Payne; I do not admit that my effort would have been more profitable as a paper than it was as an address, and I judge of this matter from the expressions of opinion as to its value which were given me by voice upon that occasion and which have been repeated by scores of letters received since.

As for members asking questions, I think the report in the *Cosmos* for May indicates that the questioning was pretty lively.

I wish to antagonize more emphatically than ever, if possible, the "*crutch*" idea as applied to gutta-percha and to insist upon just that degree of longevity for fillings of this material that I have always assumed, viz. from *twice* to *thrice* the durability of gold when used instead of gold in places which are frequently filled with gold and which *should be filled with gutta-percha*.

I deny the assertion that fillings made of the gutta-percha stoppings of the present day are inferior to those of former times; and the statement made by the gentleman that such fillings will not last longer than from two to eight years, merely because he does not happen to know any better, is "suggestive and amusing, to say the least."

I have hundreds of such fillings made from such gutta-percha which are now more than ten years old and which, with the exception of very trifling wear, are as good as when introduced and which are saving the soft, frail teeth perfectly.

In my experience the average of well introduced good gutta-percha work of the last decade is equel to, if not superior to, that of thirty years ago; therefore, the inference that such results are obtained is *neither " misleading " nor " untrue."*

It is true that I did say that it was a duty that operators should "test" their gutta-percha stopping, that from such "testing" might be known the approximate degree of heat at which it softens (as I expressed it, " its heat-grade") and also exactly its composition, (as I expressed it, " *just the proportions of* organic and inorganic matter ") and it is equally true that I said that an *analysis* was a very difficult piece of work, and the attempt to make a point on these two assertions merely because the gentleman did not happen to know the difference in gutta-percha work between " testing " and " analysing " is " suggestive and amusing, to say the least."

Regarding my assertion that the formula for "Hill's stopping," is unknown, I would say that I have, during the past twenty-five years, embraced every opportunity to ask those of our profession from whom I deemed it possible I might obtain information as to the formula of this (at first) excellent material, and, in every instance I was told by each individual that he "did not know."

It was from this fact that I said that our information was " *meagre !*"

And now I would ask further if Dr. Payne was a student with Dr. Hill, and if he made some of that material, *and if he knew* of what it was composed and *what were the proportions*, why has he not published all this long ago?

He tells us that if we used any of Hill's stopping of twenty-five years ago we used that which he made; but if my recollection serves me, it was *just about that time* that the quality of Hill's stopping commenced *markedly to deteriorate.* This might have been merely coincidental, but the reminiscence is " suggestive and amusing, to say the least."

That he thinks he knows I do not doubt, but that he knows I regard as an open question, and if it could be proven *by analysis* that he thought he knew, but did not, *it* would also be "amusing, to say the least."

Students oftentimes think they know.

I do not **see by** what authority the gentleman states that *I* know, "of course, that the best stopping in the market to-day is very much **inferior** to the article which gave the filling material its deservedly high **reputation**," *for I do not know any such thing.*

The gentleman speaks of Hill's and Bevans' stoppings, but my record of gutta-percha work was not made with either of these. I could not speak for gutta-percha with views based upon that material as given us "twenty-five or thirty years ago."

I refer to the gutta-percha *of* the **last** twenty-five **years,** with its gradual improvement in *lessened* quantity of inorganics with maintenance and *increase* of heat-grade; with its improved **toughness** and with its improved working qualities.

If the gentleman is not aware that as crude **gutta-percha** has deteriorated, gutta-percha stopping has nobly held **its** own, he should post himself before speaking, because "from such a **source of learning** and respectability we have a **right to** look for the **whole picture.**"

And so, because Hill never used steam heat, the statement that it is essential to use it now, is a " dogmatic assumption !"

Hill had the crude gutta-percha of the **cut-down trees.** We, of to-day, have only the crude gutta-percha of the tapped trees—therefore, Hill could dispense with that care and nicety of manipulation which we of to-day find *essential* to the production of an acceptable result.

It seems to me that to assume that my assertion was a dogmatic assumption is itself a dogmatic assumption !

The gentleman states that he "experimented *all one winter*" to improve the texture of the manufactured material, but he found the whole trouble was with the **base.**

I have been systematically experimenting for the same purpose *for more than twenty years,* and I feel that I have been rewarded for my labor, which, however, would only seem to indicate that I can do more in twenty years than the gentleman can in "one winter"—which I guess is true !

Second, for Dr. Bogue ; after having, in a paper on "Filling Materials and Methods," asked questions, given answers and drawn deductions just such as would have been accepted twenty years ago, but which I think would be seriously questioned in discussions of the present day, the gentleman kindly covers me over with dental sweetness and then swallows me!

Truly Bogue-ish—and as such a position is not agreeable to me I shall strive to bring about a repetition of the history of Jonah and the whale.

The jaws open with this, as if quoting from me: "I regret to hear such words as these, 'I want to induce you to try these things, for certainly you must understand that you know little or nothing about plastic fillings.'"

I never said so!

What I said was this, as reported: "I want to induce you to try these things, for certainly you must understand that *from such stand-points as I offer here to-night* you KNOW little about plastic fillings," which sentiment, I think, would not be cavilled at by, at least, a majority of those present, and I firmly believe would be *most* decried only by those *least informed*.

The jaws again open wider with this: "Can we denominate as praiseworthy and strictly scientific a sentence like this, 'If *I* do not know when it is best to extract a tooth, I do not know which of you does,'" as if quoted from me!!

I never said so!

In speaking of banding together loose and shaky teeth, I said: "It has been said that teeth in this condition had better be extracted. Is it best? And if *I* do not know when it is best to extract a tooth, I ask you who of you does?"

Simply a question, and no assertion. I do not see that seeking information is *un*-praiseworthy, or that the position or question was absolutely *un*-scientific.

Again, the gentleman insinuates that I advocate the use of gutta-percha "precisely as I would use cohesive gold!" and he kindly calls *that* "enthusiasm" when the context of the report will show that *in truth* I was speaking against that kind of use of gutta-percha which would be likely to result from the idea that it was a *temporary* filling; then it was that I said that I wanted "to leave with you to-night the impression that you can work gutta-percha precisely the same as you work cohesive gold," meaning carefully, with accuracy, and with the idea that with such work it would be compensatingly permanent; and this, *I have reason to believe, was generally and thoroughly so understood*.

The gentleman next, by a series of gyrations and one utter misquotation, lengthens "ten minutes" into "half a century" (not the *slightest* connection between the statements except the placing of them together by the gentleman!) and the half century into a life-time, thus giving " not the truth, nor any part of the truth, but everything but the truth " in contradistinction to my usual method.

In " testing " gutta-percha the aim is to find out *two* things—the relativity between the organic and inorganic components, and the " heat grade " of the material tested—with these two factors one versed in gutta-percha can tell much as to the quality of his material—for those who do not know the difference between " testing " and " analyzing " it does not tell—much!

" Testing " can be done in " *ten minutes.*"

The gentleman then mixes the next two quotations and draws *his* deduction with a child-like innocence which, for New York, is refreshing!

He says that *I* say : " The only way for you to use gutta-percha successfully is to test the various materials before putting them into the mouth. It is the work of a life-time"!!!!!!!

The admiration marks are mine, but I could not help putting them there, for again,

I never said it !

After, as he quotes, urging the " testing " of the various materials (gutta-percha stoppings) before putting them in the mouth, I said: "The testing of the *value* of the various inorganics is the work of a life-time."

The whole range of amalgam remarks in which the gentleman indulged are so indicative of utter superficiality that I shall simply pass them over as beneath my notice, merely intimating that *his testing* of "amalgams that have continued to change their form for several days, sometimes shrinking, sometimes expanding," is probably about as valuable and reliable as was his " little bottle and warm water bath" experiment to determine whether or no amalgam fillings would produce mercurial ptyalism!

But when the *gentleman* not only misquotes me, but *italicizes the word* I NEVER USED *to give point to his assertion*, I think it time that I should strongly denounce such unworthy and despicably unscientific conduct.

He says that *I* said : "I do not want *my* material to be looked upon as a crutch," and comments upon this as follows; " He will, it is hoped, pardon the suggestion " (how velvety soft is the odious phraseology!) " that this society was not aware that gutta-percha was a proprietary article, and it must regard all subjects brought before it as absolutely free for discussion."

I NEVER SAID SO !

After referring to Dr. Atkinson's former endorsement of gutta-percha as a "crutch," what I *did* say is this——"I do not want it to be welcomed on any such terms as that. I do not want this material to be looked upon as a crutch. I wish it to be looked upon as a reliable friend in need!"

Thus it will be seen that as no "proprietary" word or thought was indulged in by me, all his Mephistophilish sarcasm falls harmlessly to pieces from its own rottenness, *as it has not the slightest foundation in truth to rest upon!*

Extract from *Odontological Society Report, p. 487, July Cosmos.*

The President. Gentlemen, we have Dr. Niles, of Boston, with us to-night, and we would be glad to hear from him.

Dr. E. S. Niles. This is too great a subject for one to speak upon impromptu. We have considered the subject of amalgam in the American Academy of Dental Science for the last two meetings, and I must say that the result of the discussion is rather unsatisfactory. In fact, the present information on the subject discourages me in the use of amalgam. I now speak exclusively of copper amalgam. Since I have been in practice, I have been more or less dissatisfied with these fillings, as I think we all have, and have looked forward to some day when I might take up the subject for the purpose of making some satisfactory experiments. I regard the present investigation of amalgams as superficial, for the reason that when we speak of amalgams we may refer to any number of compounds, all of which may vary in their composition.

Etc., etc. for a page or more of remarks all of which seem to indicate that when the gentleman has "experimented" he, *perhaps* (?). will know more of the "great" subject upon which he is trying to speak.

He next continues as follows: "I was going to say in regard to the distinguished professor who addressed this society at its last meeting, that I am sorry he does not tell us fully and conclusively of what his compounds are composed, and in a way that would enable us to make similar preparations for ourselves. I am sorry to say that such is not the case, as my own experiments, as well as the experiments of my brethren in Boston and other cities have proved. Some years ago, while attending school in Philadelphia, I boarded not far from Dr. Flagg's, and we used to have on the table what the mistress was pleased to call '*scrapple*.' I was very much interested to know of what it was composed, and was told it was made of bits that came from the table, into which she put eggs, pepper and various things. It might, therefore, be made of one thing one day, but of entirely different things the next. In reflecting upon this subject I have wondered whether the making of mysterious compounds in Philadelphia was confined to the manufacture of '*scrapple*' alone, or whether other combinations in that city may not have a similar origin.

"As long as the profession consent to use alloys the composition of which they are not familiar with, no complaint can be entered against those who make amalgams or 'scrapple' alloys."

What a powerful reflector!

From his not knowing "fully and conclusively" of what my compounds are composed it is evident that he has not read "Plastics and Plastic Filling," in which work he would find just what "bits that

come from the table " are best adapted for each particular kind of
" *scrapple*."

When it is remembered that " *scrapple*" is a compound of Indian
meal and pork scraps (hence its name) it would seem that some Philadelphia wag was playing upon the credulity of the *scholar from Boston*, whose thirst for knowledge would evidently have been satisfied
with the information that " *fish balls*" were composed of chicken and
turnips.

And when it is also remembered that the *scholar from Boston* is
the gentleman who conferred upon dentistry the inestimable boon of
the " hermetically sealed tubes" for the maintenance of the integrity
of phosphoric acid menstruum just *two years after* it had been experimentally proven *and taught* that such menstruum "changed" practically at the same time, whether kept in hermetically sealed bottles, ordinarily stopped bottles, or *in wide mouthed vessels open to the air!*

And when he is further recognized as the author of the exciting
Newark anecdote of the young lady who asked him " if he was from
Boston?" to which he replied that he " was from Boston," to which
she replied that she, " also, was from Boston"—so they were *both
from Boston!* it goes without question that to repel an attack from
such a source would be merely to inaugurate another " Mosquito War!"

———

I visited New York in the acceptance of cordial and repeated invitation; I took with me for presentation, the carefully prepared results of
many years of conscientious endeavor to add to the resources of our
profession in its work of doing good.

I was unconscious of having either thought, said or done anything
which was other than interesting, instructive and acceptable.

I was not only congratulated and thanked upon that occasion, but I
have since received, from there, several written acknowledgments of
interest and satisfaction.

I am accustomed to personal abuse, and I have always striven to
live above it, but I must *openly* and *decidedly* protest against such
comments and papers as those of Drs. Payne and Bogue, which with
impertinent assurance accredit me with views which I do not hold;
with knowledge which I do not acknowledge, and with fallacious
deductions from what might be admitted if I "could be induced to
answer concisely!"

And I must also say that I was not prepared to find, as I did from
the April proceedings, that I was not only left alone to fight for myself

14

(which, I am thankful I feel completely able to do.) but such vile effort was characterized as "excellent!"

Candid, fair and honorable criticism of my views I have always earnestly invited, and when by time or argument I have been proven in the wrong I have always cheerfully and thankfully acknowledged it.

But when malicious sneers, deliberately concocted mis-statements and italicized perversion of the truth are returned for kindly effort, I think the right will be conceded me to feel that, *in certain degree*, I have been foolishly "casting pearls before swine."

www.ingramcontent.com/pod-product-compliance
Lightning Source LLC
Chambersburg PA
CBHW021528270326
41930CB00008B/1144